Simple Path to Wealth: Your guide to a prosperous, free life and financial freedom.

Joseph A. John

All rights reserved. No part of this publication may be reproduced,
distributed, or transmitted in any form or by any means, including
photocopying, recording, or other electronic or mechanical methods,
without the prior written permission of the publisher, except in the case
of brief quotations embodied in critical reviews and certain other
noncommercial uses permitted by copyright law.
Copyright © (Joseph A. John), (2023).

TABLE OF CONTENTS

CHAPTER ONE: How to think about money.
CHAPTER TWO: How to build wealth.
CHAPTER THREE: Financial coach.
CHAPTER FOUR: How to save.
CHAPTER FIVE: Financial Independence.
CHAPTER SIX: IF the stock market always goes up why do people keep losing money there
CHAPTER SEVEN: Financial plan
CHAPTER EIGHT: Living debt-free
CHAPTER NINE: Asset Allocation
CHAPTER TEN: Cash in vs. Cash out
CHAPTER ELEVEN: Cash safety net.

Chapter 1:
How to think about money

Step 1: Purchase more happiness. Money and happiness do go together, but the connection is much messier than most people think. We must consider our spending decisions and the objectives we pursue far more carefully if we want to make the most of our money.

Step 2: Place a Bet on Longevity. The majority of us will live incredibly long lives, often pursuing many careers and retiring after 20 or 30 years. That has significant effects on how we manage our finances.

Step 3: Rewire your brain. We are programmed to fail as investors and savers because of the inclinations we learned from our hunter-gatherer ancestors. As a result, successful money management requires a lot of self-control, or in the lack of self-control, a certain level of self-deception.

Step 4: Think (very, really) big. We categorize our financial affairs into some different categories, considering our debts to be unrelated to our stock and bond investment mix and our insurance policies to be distinct from our bank accounts. But to properly manage our finances and choose the best trade-offs, we need to put all of these financial puzzle pieces together, with our paycheck—or lack thereof—serving as the key organizing factor.

Step 5: is to avoid losing. To improve our financial situation, we should focus more on the threats to our future financial stability and less on how to make our money grow. This does not imply that we shouldn't take risks, such as making sizable stock market investments or taking out a sizable mortgage to purchase our first home. However, we should also work to reduce potential losses to our wealth as we save and invest for the future. These deductions may seem small, like mutual fund fees and stock trading costs, or they may be substantial, like selling stocks when the market is at its lowest or becoming disabled without disability insurance. There is the potential for significant financial harm in any scenario.

Chapter 2:
How to build wealth

1. Create a plan first.

Creating a financial plan is the first step in building money. That entails devoting some time to figuring out how to set and achieve your goals.

According to Peter Cassciotta, owner of Asset Management and Advisory Services of Lee County, "creating wealth starts with a vision and a plan."

Getting a financial advisor on board is a smart way to start developing your wealth-building strategy. The cost of hiring a certified financial planner (CFP) advisor is higher, especially for individuals who are just getting started, but you are paying for their planning expertise.

A more affordable choice might be to shop around for a Robo-advisor that also provides access to financial advisors. Look at robots like Ellevest or Betterment, which offer managed investment portfolios as well as the opportunity to speak with advisors.

Related: 3 Minutes To Find A Financial Advisor

2. Establish and adhere to a budget

Although many people loathe the letter "b," budgeting is a crucial component of your wealth-building plan. Your chances of following through on your plan and reaching your financial objectives are increased when you create and stick to a budget.

Budgets also assist you in tracking where your money goes each month and in avoiding bad habits like overspending that could jeopardize your goals.

3. Establish an emergency fund

If you don't have emergency reserves, where will the money come from when the heater breaks or the refrigerator breaks? Credit cards bear the brunt of these expenditures and fees, according to Lori Gross, a financial and investment counselor at Outlook Financial Center, and subject you to exorbitant interest rates.

By creating an emergency fund, you may improve your credit and earn interest on an online savings account while also having the security of knowing you have money set aside to handle unforeseen expenses.

4. Make Your Financial Life Automated

Making investing, paying bills, and saving automatically virtually eliminates the possibility that you will forget to save money for your objectives or make debt repayment progress.

Michael Morgan, president of TBS Retirement Planning, suggests that you set up automatic deductions from your paycheck to cover each item in the amount you've planned overall for all of your goals and obligations.

He claims that this is especially helpful when it comes to investing and saving. You avoid the urge to spend money instead of saving it by doing this. Your payments will be made regularly and you won't miss the money that is being removed automatically anytime soon," he claims.

5. Control Your Debt.

You are not alone if you carry a balance from month to month. According to an Experian study, the average American is in debt to the tune of more than $90,000.

Of course, not all debt is equal; certain debts, such as mortgages, may even be seen as "positive" debt due to their generally low-interest rates and potential for wealth accumulation. Given that you'll certainly receive at least a portion of your monthly payment back when you sell, some experts even consider a mortgage repayment to be a kind of forced savings account.

However, if you keep re-financing a lot of bad debt, such as high-interest credit card bills, each month, you run the risk of jeopardizing your financial objectives. According to Gross, having a repayment strategy is crucial if you want to live a life free of debt.

If you don't know where to begin, think about adopting the debt snowball or debt avalanche payback strategies. Additionally, keep in mind that it is possible—and frequently even advisable—to reduce debt while also saving money.

Then, as your balances decrease, you'll have even more money to contribute to your investment portfolio and emergency savings.

6. Make the most of your retirement funds

Uncle Sam offers you a few various options for retirement savings, and experts advise you to use as many of them as you can. That entails contributing as much as you can to both individual retirement accounts (think 401(k)) and your employer's retirement plan (IRAs).

If you now find it difficult to contribute the maximum allowed by law, make sure you're at least saving enough to qualify for any 401(k) match offered by your employer. This means that if your employer matches contributions up to 3%, you must contribute at least 3% of your pay each pay period.

Don't give up if your initial investments aren't very large. According to Casciotta, "most of my clients invested a tidy sum over a long time." Therefore, the force of compounding aids in making these modest investments into vast quantities of money.

Consider a target-date fund or Robo-advisor, which manages a tailored portfolio of funds depending on the number of years you have till retirement if you are unsure of the best method to begin investing in your 401(k) or IRA.

7. Maintain Diversity

Consider letting go of the belief that people can only build wealth by holding highly concentrated positions, such as substantial Bitcoin holdings. A diverse portfolio with a variety of investments may both safeguard your money and put you in a position to profit even during market downturns.

According to Veronica Willis, investment strategy specialist at the Wells Fargo Investment Institute, "a diversified portfolio includes a mix of assets that may not always move in the same direction and the same magnitude at all times and is designed to help minimize volatility over time."

8. Increase Your Income

A crucial step in learning how to accumulate wealth is to invest in yourself by increasing your income, even though this is not a decision you can make at an online brokerage. The more money you make in your lifetime, the more you have to invest.

If you've been making ends meet on your current wage and get a raise, Morgan advises, "now is the ideal time to start on the path to growing wealth," whether that entails increasing your emergency fund reserves, paying down debt, or retirement contributions.

To put yourself in a position for a safe retirement, financial advisor Michael Kitces advises saving at least half of every rise you receive. This enables you to gradually raise your quality of life while protecting you from adopting living standards that you won't be able to sustain in retirement.

Schedule a meeting with your manager to discuss how you might advance in your current position if you don't believe you are eligible for a raise. You can also think about starting a side business or experimenting with passive income.

Chapter 3:
Financial coach

Any area of your life can benefit from the assistance and accountability a skilled coach can offer. And while that kind of relationship would be beneficial elsewhere, it is particularly helpful when it comes to money.

After all, managing your financial situation might be challenging. It's a synthesis of feelings, encounters, and traditional instruction. Unfortunately, there are a lot of blind spots when it comes to money. Many of us are unsure about whether we are making the best decisions. Furthermore, there isn't always an obvious method to go back on track or even know what questions to ask if we are confident that we are not.

A financial coach may be useful in this situation. A financial coach may help you increase your bank account, your self-trust, and your peace of mind while also serving as an expert, cheerleader, and accountability partner.

What is a financial coach?
A financial coach is someone who is qualified (and trusted) to examine your finances and provide ways for you to handle your money more effectively. Instead of making decisions for you, they'll put more of an emphasis on educating you about money management so you may feel more secure about achieving your financial objectives.

What is financial coaching?
A specific form of coaching called financial coaching aids in the development of money management and financial literacy abilities in clients. A financial coach, who is not a financial expert, can teach you how to make a budget, discuss money with your partner, or explore ingrained attitudes that are influencing your spending patterns.

Even while money will probably be the topic of most of your discussions with a financial coach, it's possible that you won't only talk about money. The way you feel about money may be something your coach wants to look into. They could inquire about your upbringing in terms of money, your future aspirations, or your interactions with your significant other regarding money.

Do financial coaches and financial advisors have the same roles?

Financial coaches are not required to hold any formal licenses. Financial coaching is available to anyone. Having said that, the majority of financial coaches typically have at least some financial education. They could have academic credentials, professional certifications, or years of work experience in the finance sector. Some people may decide to obtain accreditation from a non-governmental organization, such as the Association for Financial

Counseling and Planning Education (AFCPE).

The use of some titles, such as "certified financial planner" or "investment advisor," is subject to restrictions imposed by the Financial Industry Regulatory Authority (FINRA) and state/federal governments. Usually, financial counselors who work in such a capacity have a degree in finance. Financial advisers typically have a relationship with a particular business or product, unlike financial coaches who offer both coaching and guidance. Even though they might charge for advice or planning services, they frequently earn their money by selling financial products.

The advice can be expensive due to the nature of their work (and the high costs sometimes connected with in-person financial planning). Typically, to work with a financial advisor, you must have a net worth of at least $250,000.

Goals of financial coaching.

•Make a plan to reach your financial objectives after deciding what they are.

•Pay off debt, such as credit card debt or college loans

•Learn personal finance basics and how to make wise financial decisions.
Improve your credit score to achieve future financial objectives such as purchasing a home or opening a business.

•Find out what stage of retirement planning you're at and make sure you're headed in the correct direction for a secure financial retirement.

•Create an emergency fund in case of a financial disaster or job loss.

•Recognize various financial products and determine which ones are the most appropriate for you.

•Understanding how your financial situation and spending habits affect other aspects of your life will help you improve your behavior.
financial freedom.

How to find a financial coach

The AFCPE website is a fantastic place to start if you prefer to work with an independent qualified financial consultant. They keep a list of individuals who hold the Accredited Financial Counselor or Financial Fitness Coach credential.

Asking around is a great method to discover a financial coach. Your friends and family will be more than delighted to recommend someone to you if they are currently working with someone they adore. If you don't know someone, you might be able to find someone by contacting nearby companies or investment groups.

People that sell particular goods, such as life insurance or retirement plans, can also offer excellent advice if you're wanting to buy them. Regardless of their specialization or employer, they frequently have a thorough understanding of how various financial instruments interact.

It's acceptable to heed the counsel of someone offering you a product if you believe in the brand and the individual. Someone won't just force something on you because they are trying to sell you something, after all. Anyone trying to offer you a financial product, in my experience, genuinely wants you to make the most of it.

It's part of their work, so they stand to gain by forging a close bond with you (and maybe referrals!). Financial advisors are required by law to recommend goods and services that are in their client's best interests, not their own or the business's.

Chapter 4:
How to save

1. Develop financial literacy and budgeting skills

Our best advice for making quick financial gains is straightforward: Establish a budget. You can manage your money if you have control over your budget. But where do I begin?

You must learn to manage your financial flow before you can begin saving money each month. To do this, you must be aware of all of your sources of income, including any debt payments, recurring expenses, and savings contributions.

Here's how to make a budget to get started saving right away:

Over 30 days, monitor every aspect of your money. This covers all of your earnings and outlays.

To determine how much you're now able to save or how much you're overpaying each month, compare your monthly income to your monthly expenses.

Make a distinction between fixed and variable expenses in your spending. Your fixed expenditures, which include things like rent and energy payments, are often tough to change. Your variable costs also include more easily modifiable expenses like subscription services, consumables, and entertainment.

Determine any variable expenses you may start reducing to boost the amount you can contribute each month to your savings objectives.

Regularly evaluate your progress and, if required, make improvements. There are several budgeting tools available that may assist make keeping to your budget simpler if this sounds a bit daunting.

2. Pay off your debts

You should probably pay off any remaining sums on your current loans before you start saving. A debt becomes greater the more time you take to pay it off. This is because interest, which is the cost of borrowing money, keeps rising over time. Any money you manage to preserve might be destroyed if you delay paying your bills due to the interest that will accumulate.

Consider utilizing a budgeting strategy like the 50/30/20 budget to pay off debt rapidly. The 50/30/20 rule, which was developed by US senator Elizabeth Warren when she was a Harvard bankruptcy expert, gives a straightforward method for getting out of debt. As to how it operates:

Spend 50% of your income on essentials, which includes fixed expenses like rent and utility bills.
Spend 30% of your income on desires, which includes unpredictable expenses like eating out and subscription services.

Save 20 percent of your salary. In this case, if your monthly take-home pay is €2500 after taxes, you may set away €500 per month. You'll have repaid your loan of €6000 in one year.

3. Establish a special savings account.
You must keep the money you spend on necessities distinct from the money you want to save if you want to save money quickly. This entails opening a special savings account.

By doing this, you reduce the possibility that you'll have to use your savings to pay for everyday costs. Instead, it motivates you to stick to your daily spending limit while safeguarding your funds from temptation!

Automate your saving process.

Consider automating your monthly savings contributions if you have a set monthly income. This entails setting up a monthly automatic transfer from your account for everyday expenses to your savings account. You further lower your likelihood of utilizing this money to pay for everyday costs by automating your savings.

Consider making your own Rules on N26 Spaces to make saving a little simpler. You may automatically transfer funds between your primary account and your Spaces using the in-app tool called Rules. It's a fantastic "hands-off" approach to get your savings going.

5. Have your bills automated.

While we're talking about it, automating your bill payments could also be a good idea. Paying before the due date can help you avoid any extra costs since businesses usually impose late fees if you don't make your payments on time.

6. Set a spending limit on your credit card.
Wonderful advice for quickly saving money? Decide how much you are willing to spend with your credit or debit cards. This prevents you from spending too much and motivates you to review your daily expenses in preparation. Several banks provide this service.

7. Employ the envelope method for budgeting
Use Dave Ramsey's envelope budgeting method as another terrific life tip to assist you in saving money quickly. This entails withdrawing all of your monthly salary in actual cash from the bank at the beginning of each month and putting it in different envelopes.

One of your financial objectives should be represented by each of these envelopes. You will thus have envelopes for your variable expenditures and envelopes for your fixed costs (such as rent and utility bills) (e.g., clothes shopping, eating out, and groceries). You'll make sure that you keep within a certain budget for each spending category if you pay for everything with a set quantity of actual cash.

8. Reduce your rent.

One of the simplest methods to start saving a significant amount of money each month is to reduce your rent. One of the simplest ways to achieve this if you presently live alone is to opt to share a room. If you decide to live with two more roommates, your rent will be reduced to around a third of what it is now, which quickly cuts it in half.

Therefore, if you hire a second roommate and are now paying €1300 per month for a three-bedroom apartment, you would save €650 per month. Living with two people will allow you to save around €870 per month. That comes to around €10,500 a year!

Consider moving to a smaller room if you currently share an apartment. You might save a lot of money each month since rent is often set based on the size of the room being leased. Additionally, it can inspire you to reduce, which might allow you to earn a little additional money by selling your unwanted goods.

9. Reduce your utility expenses

Reducing your utility expenses is another wonderful way to save money quickly. You might find yourself pocketing quite a bit of additional money if you can lower your gas and electric bills since they make up a sizable portion of your monthly fixed expenditures. This is how you do it:

Alternate energy suppliers. You may save hundreds of euros each month by making sure you're on the most affordable tariffs available.

Replace your incandescent lights with LED ones. A normal lightbulb uses 75–85% more energy than an LED bulb, but it also lasts 15–25 times longer.

Make a smart thermostat purchase. This will intelligently regulate your central heating, perhaps saving you a ton of money.

Fix any air leaks. Your power cost may go up if there are air gaps around your windows and doors because your heaters will need to run longer to maintain the desired temperature. Instead, use pressure-sensitive weather strips to close these openings, preventing any warm air from escaping.

10. Start a secondary business

It's worthwhile to think about starting a side business if you want to significantly increase your monthly savings. This may include anything from picking up a few freelance jobs, finding a few nighttime shifts at a bar or restaurant after your office job, working as a virtual assistant, or even pet sitting.

It might be very motivating to transfer all of the income from your side jobs directly into your savings account if you have the means to do so. But watch out for burning out. Your emotional well-being is more important than striving to meet any financial objectives!

11. Terminate all unused subscriptions

For many businesses, subscriptions are the key to financial success. This is because once a consumer signs up for their service, they are less likely to cancel it—even if they barely ever use it.

This is mostly because of the sunk-cost fallacy. The sunk-cost fallacy states that it is difficult to cancel a subscription that is seldom used since you have already spent a significant amount of money on it. So, discontinuing the subscription would entail acknowledging that all of the money invested in it up to that time was a waste. However, by postponing cancellation, it seems as if there is still a potential that the service may finally be utilized.

However, few of us make the most of our subscription services. Therefore, canceling any unused subscriptions now is more cost-effective than waiting for a potential use case.

12. Try to resolve issues on your own

Try to repair everything that breaks you since this is a terrific way to save a lot of money. You can now get information online on how to repair just about anything thanks to YouTube and the internet in general. It's usually less expensive to repair these things yourself than to hire someone else to do it or replace them completely, whether it's leaking pipes or the zipper on your trousers.

13. Consider your purchase carefully.

One of the greatest obstacles to quickly saving money is giving in to immediate satisfaction. Give yourself at least three to four days to consider a big purchase before you make it. This stops the impulsive portion of your brain from gaining control. This is the part that wants to receive a rapid serotonin boost from a flashy new buy.

Consider only making large purchases after 30 days have gone if you truly want to put yourself to the test. This is a certain strategy to prevent you from making impulsive purchases. Additionally, it allows you ample time to determine whether you can find a better offer elsewhere.

14. Purchase a vehicle after a fiscal quarter.

The best times to purchase an automobile, in general, are around the end of March, June, September, and December. Why? Because most auto dealers must meet particular sales goals to qualify for cash incentives. Although these goals are defined weekly and monthly, significant incentives are awarded every three months. Because the auto dealer will be eager to meet their quarterly sales goal, you are more likely to get a better bargain on a vehicle toward the conclusion of each financial quarter.

15. Reduce your food budget

You'll be astonished at how much money you can save for a few months if you can reduce your weekly shopping spending. Planning out all of your meals in advance is one of the greatest methods to do this. This implies that you may estimate your spending amount accurately before you start shopping, lowering the likelihood that you'll spend more than you intended.

Another suggestion is to think about avoiding meat once a week. It's worth deciding to skip meat at least once a week since it's often more costly than veggies and vegetable-based goods. Over time, these modest weekly savings will increase.

Additionally, take care to observe the merchandise displayed on the lower-level shelves. Supermarkets often place their most costly goods at eye level to encourage you to spend more money while positioning their less expensive items closer to the ground to make them more difficult to see.

16. Every month, set aside a day with no purchases.

Designate one day each month where, apart from your fixed expenditures, you'll spend nothing at all to help you develop the habit of saving money. This may include choosing to mingle at the park or home, preparing all of your meals using items you already have on hand, and spending a leisurely evening reading or watching TV.

Once you're used to it, you may extend this to two days per month and even one day per week to significantly boost your monthly savings.

17. Sell whatever unneeded stuff you have.
It's worthwhile doing an inventory of all your unneeded items and selling them on an internet market such as eBay or Nextdoor if you want to start saving money for your trip right away. This not only helps in clearing up clutter, but it also has the potential to bring in some additional cash that you can use to fund your Christmas savings goal.

How to budget for objectives and important events in life
As we previously discussed, while creating a strategy to save money quickly, it might be useful to have a clear aim in mind. This objective may sometimes be as significant as

getting hitched or purchasing a home, or it may have a lesser extent.

We have a handbook to support you wherever your savings journey takes you. Take a look at some of our resources for advice on how to budget for various life events, including:

Purchasing a vehicle – There are several ways you may quickly save money for a car. Saving for a vehicle should be a bit simpler since you typically won't need to save as much as you would for a down payment on a new home.

Purchasing a home — Saving money for a down payment on a new home might seem like an improbable goal, but there are a few clever tricks you can use to quickly save a sizable sum of money.

Getting hitched Want to know how much a wedding typically costs? Check out our cost breakdown and adhere to our straightforward advice to keep it inside your wedding budget.

Having a kid – If having children is in your plans, you should be aware of the expenses involved.

Changing careers It need not affect your financial strategy for a job move to be an exciting challenge.

Going on a sabbatical – If you're considering taking a break from your job, you should make a budget and prepare ahead. Focusing on yourself may be much more gratifying if you plan.

Moving to a foreign country may be challenging, and moving fees are a major consideration. Visit our guide to learn how to make your next foreign relocation less stressful for you and your money.

Chapter 5:
Financial independence

What is financial independence?

Financial independence allows you to make decisions without being unduly concerned about how those choices may affect your finances. This is because you are financially ready for everything life throws at you—you have no debt, cash in the bank, and you're making investments for the future.

In other words, you are in charge of your finances rather than having them in charge of you. You have choices when you have financial freedom, or as we like to call it, financial serenity. You don't need to worry about whether your finances will allow you to replace your water heater or purchase groceries for a single mother who has lost her job.

How to Achieve Financial independence?
The road to financial independence is not a quick-rich scheme. Furthermore, being financially independent does not absolve you of the obligation to manage your money wisely. The exact opposite. Complete financial management is the consequence of effort, sacrifice, and patience. And the work was worthwhile!

1. Become budget-savvy
If you don't have a strategy for your money, you won't succeed. At the end of each month, you'll instead be left wondering where your money went! That is a formula for financial ruin, not financial freedom.

Without a budget, it is hard to achieve financial independence. If you don't direct your money, you'll be left wondering where it went. Before the month starts, give each dollar a task, and keep tabs on your spending all through it. You may easily change the amount in those categories if you often overspend or underspend there.

Setting up a budget is crucial to getting your money in order, but it doesn't stop there. Even after you're financially independent, you'll still create a new budget each month. Regardless of your financial situation, you must have a strategy.

Nobody ever wins the major championship game by mistake, and the same is true for achieving financial independence. The first step to intentionally accumulating wealth is budgeting. The finest budgeting tool in the world, EveryDollar, can help you start budgeting with confidence and take charge of your finances right now.

2. Eliminate debt from your life permanently.

It's time to get rid of whatever debt you may have, including credit card debt, auto loans, school loans, and leases. Why? You'll never really be financially free as long as you're giving hundreds of your hard-earned dollars in debt payments to banks and lenders each month.

Your most effective asset for accumulating money is your income. And if all you have to work with is the leftover money after paying your credit card bills and student loan repayments, you won't achieve your financial objectives.

You may create a lasting foundation for prosperity by paying off your debt. Before you start making payments on your debt, make sure you have $1,000 saved and set away for emergencies. You don't want an unforeseen expenditure to stop you in your tracks.

Budgeting usually results in individuals feeling like they were paid more, which is fantastic news for you. Spend all of that additional money until your lowest debt is paid off. then continue to roll the snowball. Although paying off debt requires a lot of effort, there is nothing quite like the satisfaction of retaining the money you earn each month.

Are you prepared to start your path toward debt freedom? Then it's time to enroll in Financial Peace University, the program that has assisted millions of individuals just like you in paying off their debt (and keeping it that way)!

3. Create financial targets

Everyone aspires to financial independence. What a wonderful dream! But a desire is all that a dream is without a purpose. Setting financial objectives, such as paying off debt or accumulating money for retirement, is crucial on your path to financial independence. They offer you a goal to strive towards.

How can you tell whether your aim is worthwhile? To establish objectives that truly work, follow these steps:

Be precise.
Set quantifiable objectives.
Set a deadline for yourself.
Ensure that these are your objectives.
Write out your objectives.
Suppose you have a strong desire to pay off your debt. Although having that objective is wonderful, it is insufficient. How much debt

do you want to eliminate? Is it $20,000? Good, we're making progress at last! What date do you want to be debt-free by? How does one year sound? Done!

Suddenly, you have a clear, attainable objective that is important to you and has a strict deadline: I want to pay off $20,000 in debt in a year. All that's left to do is put it on paper and keep it in mind while you pursue it.

4. Make wise career decisions

Your income is your most important asset for generating wealth, as we previously said. There are several factors to consider before selecting a job. Avoid remaining in a job that is a dead end, particularly if it is unhappy. Find a profession you like that also helps you achieve your financial stability objectives so you may take pleasure in the trip.

What should you thus look for? Here are some things to remember:

In ten years, where do you want to be? Consider the end when beginning. Does this position fit in with your overall objectives?
Is there a chance to make money? Make sure there is room for your income to grow as your worth rises, even if you don't start off generating your ideal pay.
Can you develop it? Exist any chances for you to grow and develop both professionally and personally?
Do you like your job? Don't work a job you despise for your whole career. Find a cause that inspires you and enables you to put your talents to work.
Do the advantages help you achieve your financial independence goals? Your alternatives for health insurance and retirement savings might have a significant

impact on your capacity to accumulate money.

Take job decisions carefully since they may have a significant influence on your long-term financial strategy. Want to know more about finding and performing employment that pays well and has a significant positive influence on the world? Check out Ken Coleman's newest book, From Paycheck to Purpose: The Clear Path to Doing Work You Love, which is a best-seller and career expert!

5. Save the cash for unforeseen expenses

You need a fully loaded emergency fund if financial independence is your ultimate objective. It serves as a barrier between you and unforeseen life events like auto repairs, broken appliances, and medical deductibles that affect all of us. As a result, after you're debt-free, you should raise your emergency fund to pay for three to six months' worth of costs.

You'll feel more secure if you have the money on hand to deal with an unforeseen life crisis, and having this money is essential to your entire financial strategy. You'll notice that your budget has more wiggle room after your savings account is filled. You won't feel any remorse at all when you say "yes" to specialty lattes and extravagant shopping!

6. Make Big Purchase Plans
You'll also need a savings strategy since you won't be taking on debt for major expenditures that aren't emergencies. Take your summer vacation, for instance. It's easy! Divide the entire cost of your trip by the number of months you have to save as a line item in your monthly budget. Your debt-free status allows you to enjoy your trip

without worrying about a credit card payment when you get home.

You'll have the financial base to begin investing after you have a fully funded emergency fund and a strategy in place to pay for large expenditures.

7. Make investments for your retirement.
You're prepared to work with a financial adviser who can help you make the most of your long-term investing alternatives now that you have a strategy for short-term savings. The good news is that your money will have more time to grow the earlier you start investing. That is the compound growth principle in action. How to begin going is as follows:

Start by using the tax-favored retirement plans you have access to at work, such as your 401(k) or 403(b) (b). Eight out of ten billionaires, according to The National Study of Millionaires, invested in their company's 401(k) plan, which was crucial to their financial success.

How much should you put aside? Spend 15% of your salary on retirement investments. And if your company matches your 401(k) contributions, take advantage of it! Never turn down free money.

It's excellent if your employer offers a Roth 401(k) with reputable mutual fund choices. You may put all 15% of your money there. If you have a standard 401(k), however, invest up to the match and then put the remaining 15% into a Roth IRA. Return to your 401(k) if you still have any of your 15% available after maxing out a Roth IRA (k).

Why is a Roth a wise decision? The money you put into a Roth 401(k) or Roth IRA grows without paying taxes. In other words, when you take money out of retirement, you don't have to pay taxes on it. That is a significant advantage that you shouldn't pass up.

8. Look for methods to save costs.
It's time to examine your spending patterns if you haven't taken a close look at just what you're spending your money on each month.

It's simple to get caught up in everyday life and forget about the gym membership you bought at the start of the year but haven't been in a while. Or all those subscriptions to streaming services you made even though you only watch a few hours of television every week.

Here are a few suggestions for immediate cost savings:

Overname brands, choose generics.
Plan your meals and bring leftovers to work.
At home, make your coffee.
Pause or cancel memberships and subscriptions.
Boost energy efficiency.
Utilize discounts and cashback applications.
And what's this? More than 93% of millionaires continue to utilize coupons to save money on their purchases even after they've attained financial independence. 1 It seems that conserving money is a difficult habit to break.

9. Budget Your Money

You must, in other words, live on less money than you earn. This complements having a budget well. To achieve financial independence, you must have self-control and be ready to turn down those things you can't now afford to save more money over time.

We're not saying it's terrible to desire good things or to have them, so listen up. Simply put, we don't want your things to have you. You'll continually find yourself stuck in the vicious cycle of debt and overspending if you spend money you don't have on that home or vehicle to impress people you don't even like. That is not a plan for achieving financial security. In actuality, the reverse is true.

10. Assist Your Children with College Savings

You may begin saving for your children's education expenses by opening an Education Savings Account if you are currently putting 15% of your salary into retirement (ESA).

The money you put into an ESA grows tax-free, similar to a Roth IRA, so you won't have to pay taxes on it when you use it to pay for college. Currently, you are allowed to make an ESA contribution for each kid up to $2,000 per year. Income restrictions are in place, and your financial advisor can help you determine if they apply to you.

Speak to your financial adviser about a 529 plan if you wish to save more than you can with an ESA (or if you aren't eligible to make contributions). Moreover, these programs grow tax-free! Just be aware that you should steer clear of some 529 programs. Avoid fixed investment alternatives and prepaid tuition programs.

The benefit of laying aside money for your children's education is that you're preparing them for financial independence by assisting them in avoiding student loan debt.

11. Early mortgage repayment

There is a good reason why the typical billionaire pays off their home in about 10 years.

What would your life be like if you didn't have a mortgage payment? The grass just feels different when you own your home instead of a bank or mortgage lender. Money freedom is what freedom looks like.

You might pay off your home years earlier and avoid paying tens of thousands of dollars in interest by making an additional payment every quarter. To determine how to reduce your mortgage term, utilize our mortgage payback calculator.

12. Put your health first.

Everyone is aware of the benefits of eating well and exercising often for good health. What if, however, we informed you that leading a healthy lifestyle also benefits your money account?

There is little question that America is now experiencing a health catastrophe. Furthermore, if you do nothing to improve your health, it might cost you your financial independence. This is because greater health issues result in more doctor visits and medical expenses, which raise insurance rates.

Treatment for certain illnesses brought on by a bad diet costs roughly $300 per person per year or $50 billion on a national scale.

And around one in ten persons in the United States now have some kind of medical debt, which equates to 23 million people and a debt of over $200 billion. 6

You may also take care of your financial health when you take care of your physical, emotional, and spiritual well-being. Different research discovered that American people might save $88.2 billion in costs if they adopted a healthy diet by reducing their risk of developing heart disease, cancer, Type 2 diabetes, and Alzheimer's disease. 7

13. Set up the appropriate insurance.
What does insurance have to do with having financial independence, you may be wondering. a lot! Sports teams that win championships don't simply concentrate on their attack; they also have a good defense.

Insurance serves as a protective measure to safeguard your cash.

Without the proper insurance, one unfortunate incident or one court case might jeopardize all you've fought so hard to achieve. Financial independence may be attained via budgeting, saving, and investing; but, it can also be maintained through insurance.

Here are eight forms of insurance that you must have:

Long-term care insurance
vehicle insurance
Renters' and homeowners' insurance
health protection
insurance for long-term disability
insurance for long-term care
preventing identity theft

umbrella coverage

Want assistance? Your best option is to speak with a RamseyTrusted insurance specialist who can assist you in locating the finest offers for the precise level of insurance you want.

14. Utilize a financial advisor

It could seem intimidating to actively choose how to manage your finances and assets. You are not alone if you feel that way.

Don't leave your financial future to chance, you've worked hard to build the correct foundation. To manage your investment alternatives and endure the ups and downs of the stock market, you need the knowledge of a financial adviser.

Your financial counselor can:

Make choices on your investing approach.
Regularly rebalance your investments to reduce risk
Make a realistic strategy for what your level of financial independence will be.
Know about other financial alternatives than retirement funds.
Create a withdrawal strategy tailored to your scenario.

15. Generousness toward others
Being able to handle unforeseen emergencies—like a vehicle repair—without breaking a sweat is just one aspect of financial independence. When you acknowledge your capacity to address others' needs, the fun truly begins. Imagine providing for a family in need by covering their automobile maintenance costs! The

focus has changed from being all about you to leave a legacy.

The nice thing is that being kind doesn't have to wait till you're financially independent. Even whether you're focused on consolidating debt or increasing your emergency fund, we always advise starting your budget with a line item for charitable contributions. At that point, your donations may seem like tithes to a local church or nonprofit organization. However, after you've achieved financial independence, that's when you can truly let your generosity run wild!

If you live uniquely, you may also give uniquely in the future. All the effort it takes to get it is worthwhile. You can do this.

Chapter 6:
If the stock market always goes up why do people keep losing money there

However, it's common to see individuals there daily losing money. According to certain research, 90% of investors, both new and experienced, have lost money in this market, while 95% of Indian day traders lose money there every day.

If we want to be investors, this prompts us to address the crucial question, "If the stock market is continually going up, why do people keep losing money there?" What drives an investor to sell at a loss, especially given that we are all aware that we don't lose money unless we sell?

Here's what you need to know about why investors lose money in the market despite evidence to the contrary and how you can apply these lessons to shield your portfolio from loss.

•They are using funds that they may want later.
Even if the market is down 50% if you don't sell your stocks, you won't be that much worse off; rather, you'll just be going through a rough patch. The issue arises when you have to sell because of life's circumstances and you need the money you have on hand.

Most individuals lose money in this area. When something happens, they are forced to sell their investments at a loss because they thought they had found a good investment opportunity and had used all of their capital to make a profit.

Simply not using the money you know you will need later can resolve this problem. Instead of investing money that will be used to fix your garage in six months, invest money that you can live without for five to ten years.

I register market-related cash as an expense when I use it. In this manner, I can put exactly the right amount of money there and carry out the rest of my financial plan without any problems.

•They lack a well-thought-out plan.
The majority of individuals advocate an investment strategy centered on stock funds. For 35 years, they invest $500 each month in the S&P 500, and at the end of that time, they will have $1,000,000 invested there.

Other investors choose certain stock categories, such as dividend foundation stocks, growth companies, or tech firms, and invest a certain percentage of their capital in each one. Others, in addition, invest a large portion of their funds in ETFs.

The key message is that, as long as you use one, there is no ideal investing approach. However, if you just enter the market to place your money there without having a strategy in place, you will lose money since you won't be aware of your objectives while making a deal.

- They pay no attention to world events or market cycles.

Most individuals conflate long-term price patterns with short-term volatility. When the market is booming, this confusion forces them to sell everything to stop additional harm.

The growth and fall of business and economic cycles. The majority of movements also rely on world events.

Before an investment reaches $1000, it will first reach $700, then return to $500, and maybe halt for a time at $800. Most people anticipate that something would go from one place to another in a straight line, but when that doesn't happen, they get impatient and opt to sell to seize faster possibilities.

•As novices, they make margin purchases.
When I first began trading, I experienced this. I discovered that, with only $200 of my funds, I could execute transactions worth $1,000 because of the leverage certain platforms provide.

Nevertheless, since the platforms stopped my transactions when the price fell too far, I lost all of my starting cash because I lack expertise in forecasting ups and downs.

The fact that margin doesn't let you fail is one of its fundamental flaws. Platforms compel you to sell at a loss if they lose money, and sometimes large deals cause your capital to be as little as $0.50 down.

Many novice investors think that using margin would help them grow their initial portfolio more quickly, but if you don't know the market well, I think it might work against you. Particularly because with margin, you only have one chance to succeed but without it, you may make as many errors as you want and if you don't sell, you won't lose.

- They purchase an illogical item.

Sometimes owning something won't result in financial gain. You must be aware of which stocks are worthwhile holding.

For instance, Peloton stock dropped from more than $100 a share in 2021 to $8.51 today, and it is not anticipated that it will ever rise to that level again as a result of the CEO's poor choices. However, given that the businesses that sell home goods were at their height in 2020, it could have been a wise investment.

Currently, if you acquire a Peloton share knowing all the firm did to lose every penny of its cash, that decision would be absurd. However, the majority of investors only consider the "potential profit" they could realize if the stock returns to its all-time high, and that is when they end up losing money.

Make sure you know why you are buying anything rather than just if it is in style at the moment. Even if a deal doesn't go as planned, you can still have a potential stock that might eventually result in a profit.

•Final reflections
Many individuals may think it's difficult to avoid losing money in the stock market, but it only takes discipline, the correct attitude, and adhering to a strategy. If you know the steps to take to be profitable, as long as you do those steps, you will always be successful.

Follow these easy steps if you want to avoid losing money in the stock market and develop wealth over time with it:

Squander just the money that you won't need in the next five or ten years; don't use money that will be needed to repair your residence in a month.

Create a portfolio of high-quality companies that you are certain will perform well in the long run, rather than just those you believe would increase your wealth immediately.

If you are inexperienced, avoid making margin purchases since you only have one shot at it.

Purchase only sensible items, such as reliable businesses and forward-thinking initiatives, and avoid fad stocks and business ventures.

CHapter 7:
Financial plan

A financial plan is a detailed outline of your financial objectives and the actions you must take to reach them. To make sure that a financial plan is definite and definitive, it is often documented in tangible papers. Since investing is often a component of a financial plan that can help you save for the future, many individuals combine their financial plan with an investment strategy. A financial plan should also include an estate plan, a college savings plan, a retirement plan, and other vital components.

A Financial Plan: What Is It?

Your financial objectives are identified, arranged, and prioritized in a financial plan, which also lays out the activities you must take to accomplish them. They may also help you determine if you need to make changes to your spending or whether you're on pace to accomplish your financial objectives. These strategies might center on debt consolidation, opening a brokerage or bank account, starting a savings routine, or developing an investing strategy.

Depending on the duration of your objectives, financial plans might span years, months, or even decades. However, by taking a few little efforts, such as setting a monthly savings target or investing some of your income, your financial plan may result in far better future planning.

Financial plans are often adaptable as well, making room for any unanticipated circumstances or potential life changes. A long hospital stay, a marriage, the birth of a child, a relocation, a new job, and other life events may fall under this category.

What Makes Up a Financial Plan's Core Elements?

To make your financial strategy as successful as possible, you should put a lot of thought into it for you and your family. You will need to consider several parts of your financial life, such as your tax returns, retirement funds, and investments, to accomplish this effectively.

A sound financial plan often includes several essential components. Although each of them has a unique impact on your finances, taken together, they determine how your finances will develop in the future. The following are the financial groups and subgroups to pay attention to:

What Makes Up a Financial Plan?
Budgeting - A cash flow statement that details your sources of revenue and outgoing costs - Review your assets and liabilities on a balance sheet. both the advantages and disadvantages of your present financial status
– Plan for financing education

Asset allocation strategies, investment portfolio return statistics, and an overview of retirement account investments

Retirement planning, estimations of post-retirement income, including Social Security, and a post-retirement lifestyle plan

Planning for philanthropic gifts, estate/inheritance tax calculations, and a will that has been executed

Capital gains and income tax returns; 401(k) and IRA contribution plans; tax planning

Risk management, long-term care insurance, disability insurance, and life insurance, as well as annuities.

How to Make a Financial Plan in Steps

The majority of individuals have a variety of short- and long-term financial objectives, such as debt repayment, retirement preparation, and student fund development. Each financial plan, however, will change somewhat since each person's specific circumstance is distinct. However, there are generally five stages that must be taken to create a thorough financial plan:

Establish your financial objectives.
Gather any pertinent records and account statements that provide insight into your present financial position.
To achieve your financial objectives, create both a short- and long-term strategy.
Start implementing your financial strategy.
As your life and ambitions change, modify your financial strategy.

Step 1: Describe your financial objectives
The first step in creating a financial strategy is to decide precisely what you want to achieve. Start by going through potential short- and long-term objectives. One of them may be making a down payment on a

home, clearing your debt, or purchasing a brand-new vehicle. These objectives will serve as the main inspiration for your financial strategy.

Outlining these objectives should take your financial future into account as a whole. Don't simply concentrate on one part of your money since everything is related. When it comes to family planning, for instance, you may want to consider both creating a college savings fund and making a down payment on a property.

Step 2. Gather data on your finances and investments.

You may start an analysis of your financial status once you've set objectives and requested support if you need it. Include any financial obligations and assets, such as loans, investments, retirement accounts, and real estate. It is possible to have a more precise knowledge of your present financial situation by analyzing all of this data.

Start with constant things like your rent or mortgage, utility bills, and other set costs while gathering information. To determine how much you typically spend on items like food, entertainment, vacation, clothing, etc., look back at your spending history. Of course, you'll also want to be aware of all of your revenue sources, including your salary as well as any rental or investment income.

Knowing where you are right now can assist you to decide what actions to do next to reach your objectives. Based on your starting place, you may adjust your objectives or schedule to make them more realistic and doable.

Step 3: Create a comprehensive financial plan.
You may begin creating the concrete phases of your financial plan after you have

determined your financial situation and objectives. This will probably include setting aside funds for retirement, an emergency fund, or a significant purchase. Your financial strategy will probably include a significant amount of investment since, in the long run, it is the greatest method to increase your wealth.

Your personal preferences and risk tolerance will determine the precise manner in which you invest. A financial adviser can assist you in choosing the ideal mix of major and small-cap stocks, bonds, cash, and alternative assets based on your interests.

If buying a home or a new automobile is one of your objectives, your strategy should also contain actions to improve your credit. If you already have a good credit rating, you won't need to do anything. However, if your credit score isn't where it ought to be, part of your strategy should center on promptly making payments on your credit card and student loan balances as well as other ways to establish credit.

Last but not least, paying off your debt will be a component of your strategy if you have a lot of it. Your specific course of action will depend on your circumstances, including whether you decide to apply for a consolidation loan or not, whether to raise your monthly payment or not, etc.

By making suggestions based on your financial overview, a financial adviser may assist you with the financial planning process. They are there to assist, whether it is by recommending a minimum amount to save or a schedule for paying off debt. Consider any dangers or alternatives they suggest. These procedures might help you avoid getting in a bind if your financial strategy ever has to be modified.

Step 4: Put Your Financial Plan Into Practice in Your Daily Life

It's time to execute your strategy when you've made it. Instead of diving right in, it can be simpler to make a modest first investment. For instance, start saving in little amounts rather than saving half of your income all at once.

Your financial plan's timescale can be years long, so there might not be any immediate benefits. But if you follow the stages specified in your strategy, you'll get there quickly.

It's crucial to carry out the actions outlined in your financial strategy. However, it's also crucial to acknowledge that unforeseen events do occur, from beginning a new job to experiencing a medical emergency. Any unforeseen circumstance might affect your money, so you should adjust your strategy as necessary. It will more accurately represent your financial situation this way.

Step 5: Refresh Your Long-Term Financial Plan Regularly

Of course, monetary fluctuations might make it more difficult for you to achieve your financial objectives. After these unforeseen obstacles, you should review your strategy to determine whether you can still achieve your objectives. If not, changing the plan is simple. You may adjust the deadline, increase the minimum amount you must save, or modify the objective entirely.

It might be beneficial to consult with your financial counselor every few months. They can assist you in making adjustments to your strategy if required to help you get back on track. When it comes to changing your strategy in response to new goals or failures, be flexible and transparent with your adviser.

How to Create a Financial Plan

Having a professional's assistance may be quite helpful since financial planning can get complicated. Financial advisers often provide services for financial planning and, if necessary, investment guidance. You may interview your advisor matches for free to choose which one is best for you using SmartAsset's free service, which connects you with up to three local financial advisers. Start your search for a financial adviser right away if you're prepared to do so.

Do you want to begin making your investments? Open a brokerage account first, then choose an asset allocation based on your particular risk appetite. Your investment may be made simpler by using a Robo-advisor service, which makes recommendations based on proprietary algorithms.

Chapter 8:
Living debt free

The typical American household spends 20% of their income, according to the United States Federal Reserve Board, on debt payments.
These payments cover both mortgage and consumer debt.

A realistic long-term financial plan must contain a repayment schedule so that you may pay off your debt and accomplish your savings target at the same time. Your capacity to survive on less money grows significantly if you are debt-free. Keep in mind that you must earn both the debt payment amount and the income taxes necessary to pay the debt in order to pay it off. The typical American household spends about 30% of every dollar earned to settle their debts each year after adding the taxes due on income.

I usually suggest paying your debts in the order shown below when choosing which to do first: Debt that is not tax deductible is greater than debt associated with a home mortgage.

Because the interest on your house is often tax deductible but the interest on credit card debt and other consumer debt is typically not, you may choose to pay off your mortgage debt.

Four steps of living debt free:

1. Begin modestly. No of the sum or interest rate, you should prioritize paying off any modest, easily repayable obligations first. A feeling of success and the elimination of monthly payments that come with paying off a loan early might help you stay dedicated to your goal of living debt-free.

2. Understand Your Rates. Sort your loans from highest to lowest interest rate first.

Prioritize the order in which you should pay them off using the interest rates. Sort your debt according to fixed and variable rates. In most circumstances, variable rates should be prioritized above fixed rates.

3. Think about the term. Place open-ended liabilities ahead of loans with defined terms. For instance, the length of a vehicle loan is normally set. If you pay your bill on time, you will repay the loan within the allotted period. However, a credit card has no term. A portion of your amount is used as your payment. Making simply the minimal payment will thus result in years of interest payments.
Dad and son

4. The Bottom Line on Tax Benefits. Loans like mortgages, home equity lines of credit, and student loans often come with tax advantages. Those should be less of a priority to pay off than obligations like

credit cards or auto loans. Place them at the end of the list.

Start at the top of your list now that it has been prioritized. Your maximum debt payment should be applied to the first loan on your list. Pay the bare minimum on all of your loans after the first. Congratulate yourself and move on to the next item on your list when you've finished paying off your first debt. Up until you reach your first mortgage, if applicable, you should continue making your top loan's maximum debt payment.

Characteristics of debt-free living

1. They are anticultural

These folks are aware that taking on debt won't be a winning strategy. According to society, you need a credit card to thrive, student loans are a must for attending college, and you'll constantly owe money on your automobile. These are outright lies.

People who are living debt-free do not adhere to these conventions. Their daily existence does not need credit cards. Their finances are not significantly affected by car payments. They quickly get rid of their debt, treating it like the week-old meatloaf they discovered in the back of their refrigerator. Debt is typical. So be strange!

2. They exercise restraint.
Adults establish plans and adhere to them, claims Dave Ramsey. Kids act according to their feelings. A person with a strong desire to pay off their debt may resist the urge to make an impulsive purchase and walk right by the shoe aisle with the huge discount or the flat-screen TV aisle.

They don't purchase things just because they desire them or because they're on sale. They are intelligent enough to understand that making purchases won't solve all of their concerns or ultimately make them feel better.

Debt-free individuals avoid making purchases until they have the means to do so. They are prepared to patiently wait, labor, and save.

3. They exude assurance.

Someone confident in their financial strategy doesn't care what other people think of them. They don't mind driving an outdated vehicle since there are no payments to be made. They don't have to spend a lot of money on holidays to share beautiful pictures on social media. In addition to brand names, they also check price tags. Why? They no longer strive to keep up with the Joneses who live next door.

And what's this? This type of unwavering self-control leaves more money available to pay off their obligations. They get more and more confident as they pay off debts.

4. They don't hesitate to refuse.
If you're continuously saying yes to every social invitation that comes your way, it's difficult to maintain a debt-free existence. It's crucial to retain the word "no" in your vocabulary, whether it's for a shopping trip, vacation, dining out with friends, or simply spending money on a whim.

5. They make objectives.
Simple enough, right? Living debt-free is a goal, therefore those who desire to achieve it keep that aim in mind. They establish written, personally owned, time-sensitive, explicit, quantifiable objectives for you.

They decide what they want to achieve and then create a plan to make it happen.

6. They have gazelle intensity.

You undoubtedly recall Dave talking about gazelle intensity if you have taken Financial Peace University. It occurs when you get so depressed about your debt that you sprint away from it (like a gazelle). This indicates that they are trying to eke out every last dollar from their budget. They are using coupons, searching for deals wherever they go, and even working a second job. Everyone has joined.

7. They are unconcerned about things.

People who are materialistic place too much value on "things." They take on an absurd amount of debt to pay for holidays, expensive automobiles, and even large homes.

But those who are motivated to pay off their debt are aware that happiness cannot be purchased with money. With what they have, they are happy.

8. They're prepared to give up something.
A person may have to refrain from spending money on items like eating out, weekly movie dates, and the premium television package while working toward debt freedom. But bear in mind that spending reductions are just temporary. The budget will have more flexibility for that dinner and movie outings after the debt is paid off.

9. They are incomparable.
The lifestyles of debt-free individuals are not compared to others nearby or on social media. They are aware that they are on their road, pursuing their objectives and aspirations. They are happier and happier

with their life as a result of not comparing themselves to others.

10. They are giving.
Debt-free people are aware of their freedom to live and offer. They are aware that they may have more fun with money the more they keep their hands open. It's always more enjoyable to donate to a greater cause than to save that money for oneself, whether they are supporting family, friends, church, or a mission they believe in. Giving is the greatest joy you'll ever have with money, according to Rachel Cruze. Test it out for yourself.

Winning ways to become debt free:

1. Build up your emergency fund

Numerous people get themselves into debt by borrowing money from others to meet sudden requirements that arise after they prepare their budgets. If certain exceptions are established, a situation like this may be avoided. Over urgent financial contingencies, saving up for an emergency has an edge.

2. Eliminate unnecessary spending

People may incur debt to fulfill their desire for other goods they cannot afford. A large portion of these urges is unneeded pleasures. When getting ready to get out of debt, all unnecessary expenses may be stopped. It is critical to provide basic requirements priority.

3. Create a refunding timetable.

Paying off debts may feel overwhelming, especially if they build up over time. However, this may be expedited by adhering to a repayment plan where the debt is divided into affordable payments for a certain term. This action would lessen the strain of using up all money or revenue to pay off debts, which normally demotivates people. To pay off debts fast, it's important to make a strategy for repayment and to keep track of the progress accomplished.

4. Boost your earnings

It might be difficult to pay off debts when you have a poor earning capacity. Such a person may borrow money or incur debt regardless of the financial plans they have established if their income is insufficient to cover their demands. It is advised to start new habits to increase one's income to avoid this. This can include taking on a second job or making money from one's skill or expertise.

5. Prevent reasons for unforeseen expenses

A person should avoid behaviors or activities that might lead to spending over their means if they want to pay off their debt. When creating plans to pay off debts, activities like shopping, going out with friends, and other things that seem to encourage impulsive spending should be avoided.

6. Make an expense plan

One of the main causes of debt traps for individuals is impulsive shopping. People prefer to spend their money on attractive and desired things rather than on necessities like food and shelter. To maintain a debt-free existence, expenses should be properly planned and analyzed. By doing this, impulsive purchases and debt accumulation may be avoided.

7. Manage your finances responsibly

Effective regulation of revenues and spending is required. If you don't accept responsibility for your money, you can't get out of debt. It would be beneficial if you were more responsible for how and what you spend your money on. Being financially responsible entails managing your finances sensibly and taking responsibility for your money.

Living debt-free is not simple since it calls for much planning, preparation, and attention to detail. However, the aforementioned advice will show you how to live a debt-free life.

Chapter 9:
Asset allocation

What is asset allocation

By distributing assets across main categories including cash, bonds, stocks, real estate, and derivatives, asset allocation is a strategy for balancing risk in investment portfolios. Each asset class will react differently over time since each has a distinct amount of return and risk.

Things to know about asset allocation

1. Return vs. Risk

The asset allocation process revolves around the risk-return tradeoff. Everyone may easily claim they want the largest return possible, but the solution isn't as simple as picking the assets with the most potential, such as stocks and derivatives.

1929, 1981, 1987, and more recent drops that occurred between 2007 and 2009 during the global financial crisis are all instances of periods when choosing equities with the largest prospective returns was not the best course of action. It's time to accept the fact that every year, another investor, mutual fund, pension plan, etc. will outperform you in terms of returns. The capacity to balance risk and return is what sets successful investors apart from greedy and return-hungry ones.

Yes, riskier investors should invest more of their funds in equities. But you should reduce your exposure to stocks if you can't stay invested through a bear market's brief volatility.

2. Programs and Schedule Sheets
Although financial planning tools and survey forms created by financial advisers or investment businesses might be useful, you should never depend completely on them.

One outdated rule of thumb, for instance, is to deduct the client's age from 100 to establish the percentage that should be allocated to equities. For example, if you are 35 years old, you should invest 65% of your money in stocks and the remaining 35% in bonds, real estate, and cash. The recommendation nowadays is 110 or even 120 minus your age.

However, typical spreadsheets sometimes fail to account for other crucial details like whether or not you are a parent, retiree, or spouse. Sometimes the questions on these forms are straightforward and don't adequately reflect your financial objectives.

Keep in mind that financial institutions like to lock you into a conventional plan because it's convenient for them rather than because it's best for you. People may obtain a general idea from rules of thumb and planner

102

sheets, but don't limit yourself to what they say.

3. Understand Your Goals

We all have objectives. You should include it in your asset-allocation strategy whether your goals are to accumulate a sizable retirement fund, buy a boat or vacation house, support your child's education, or just save for a new automobile. When choosing the ideal blend, all of these objectives must be taken into account.

For instance, you won't need to be concerned with short-term stock market swings if you want to acquire a beachfront retirement apartment in 20 years. But you may need to shift your asset allocation to safer fixed-income assets if you have a kid who will start college in five or six years. Additionally, you may want to switch to a larger ratio of fixed-income assets to stock holdings as you get closer to retirement.

4. Your Best Friend Is Time

According to the U.S. Department of Labor, you must save three times as much each month to catch up for every 10 years you put off investing for retirement or another long-term goal.

With time, you may invest more of your portfolio in greater risk/return assets, like equities, as well as take advantage of compounding and the time value of money. In 30 years, a handful of poor stock market years will probably be little more than a distant memory.

5. Simply Do It!

The moment has come to put your chosen stock, bond, and investment combination into practice. Discovering the structure of your present portfolio is the first step.

It's quite simple to see how much of your assets are in stocks as opposed to bonds but don't forget to classify your stock holdings by small, mid, or big size. Additionally, you want to group your bonds into short-, medium-, and long-term maturity categories.

Mutual funds may provide extra difficulties. Sometimes fund names don't provide the whole picture. To learn where the assets of the fund are invested, you must go further into the prospectus.

Steps to choosing the right asset allocation

1. Choose your objectives.

Your asset allocation decision is influenced by your investing objectives. The goal is to choose assets that will most likely help you reach your goals without putting you in unnecessary danger.

The first step is to decide what you want to achieve. Both long-term and upcoming ambitions may fall under this category. Everyone's will be different, but some typical investing objectives are as follows:

Increasing your retirement fund
Increasing your children's college fund
saving for a down payment on a house
putting aside money for house improvements
obtaining start-up funds for a new venture or profession
Your investing horizon will likely play a significant role in retirement savings. This objective may be focused on by being aware of the recommended savings amount by age.

2. Recognize various asset classes
Investigating various asset types comes next. Imagine them all as umbrellas. You

may add the assets listed below to your investing portfolio. They each have potential advantages as well as hazards (more on this in a minute). The three major asset classes are broken out in the table below:

Stocks: These are ownership interests in publicly listed businesses that you may buy on the stock market. You may acquire ownership in these businesses by purchasing shares. You may sell your shares for a profit if the price increases. One method is to purchase individual shares, or you may choose to purchase tiny shares of many companies via a mutual fund or exchange-traded fund (ETF).

Bonds: In essence, they are loans. By purchasing a bond, you're lending money to the business or government entity that issued it. Then, you'll get a repayment with interest over time. Bonds, bond mutual funds, and bond ETFs are all offered via brokers. Additionally, you may buy Treasury and municipal bonds straight from the issuer.

Cash: When investing in certain asset types, liquidity might be a problem. If you're under the age of 59 1⁄2, for instance, and you want to withdraw money from your 401(k), there will be a 10% penalty. Furthermore, you are depriving yourself of potential investment gains. Having cash on hand might help with unexpected expenses and provide some assurance of income in retirement. A high-yield savings account will probably provide the most return.

A note on possible returns: According to J.P. Morgan, the S&P 500 generated an average annualized return of 7.5% from 2001 to 2020. Bond returns on average were 4.8%. In terms of cash, a high-yield savings account now offers a competitive APY of 0.70%.

3. Consider Your Tolerance for Risk

A certain amount of risk must be accepted to choose the ideal asset combination. You should probably allocate a part of your portfolio to stocks since they are often essential to provide the type of returns that will support long-term, sustainable growth. One of the main ways to stay up with inflation is via stocks.

Bonds are just as significant. Although they provide smaller returns than stocks, bonds are typically thought of as safer investments that may give your portfolio stability and more consistent income.

Similar to the yin and yang of your investment portfolio, stocks, and bonds. How much should you thus allot to each? It primarily depends on your age. One general rule of thumb is to own 60% equities and 40% bonds since this has traditionally provided steady returns. According to

Vanguard research, this kind of portfolio had an average yearly return of 9.1% from 1926 to 2020. Having said that, it's generally a good idea to tip the scales in favor of less hazardous assets as you get closer to retirement.

In addition to the risk connected with stocks and bonds, having too much cash may also be risky. Your money isn't working as hard for you as it might when it's not invested. You will probably be shut off from future investment gains and find it challenging to keep up with inflation if you retain the majority of your nest egg in a savings account.

Alternative investments should also be taken into account. Consider cryptocurrencies, private equity, hedge funds, and real estate. They deviate from the three major asset groups and often involve more risk. They may also provide substantial profits. It's all a balance, to reiterate.

4. Start Allocating Resources

The work then shifts to selecting assets after looking into several asset classes and comprehending the possible risks and rewards of each. What you need is a combination of assets that balances your portfolio while advancing your objectives.

The 60/40 portfolio has long been recognized as a recommended asset allocation, as was already said, but it doesn't imply it's appropriate for everyone. Younger people who are further from retirement can think about increasing their portfolio's level of risk. They have greater time to recover from market turbulence because of their long time horizon. On the other hand, those who are getting close to retirement don't have that luxury. If they have a portfolio that is heavily weighted in stocks at this point, a market drop might significantly reduce their worth.

It might be challenging to choose the ideal asset allocation for your age. While doing it alone is absolutely an option, working with a knowledgeable financial advisor may help remove some of the uncertainty. Based on your objectives, level of risk tolerance, and time horizon, they ought to be able to provide tailored advice.

In any case, it's typically advised to rebalance your portfolio once a year. Your asset allocation may veer off course as a result of the frequent market action changing the prices of your assets. Rebalancing entails reorganizing your portfolio and reestablishing the allocation you had originally planned.

How should you choose your asset allocation

1. If feasible, start building up a cash reserve inside your retirement plan five years before retiring (money market funds, CDs) (to defer taxes on interest). By the time you retire, you should aim to have saved enough money to cover your living costs for four years, less any pension and Social Security benefits you may get.

2. Your four-year cash reserve plus properly managed stock mutual funds should make up your retirement portfolio. Take your withdrawals for living costs exclusively from your stock mutual funds if the stock market is up (at or pretty near to its historically high level), and keep doing so for as long as the market is generally stable or continues to

grow. Do not respond to brief, small up- or down-trends. (As you do this, be sure to periodically withdraw money from various equity mutual funds to maintain your allocation percentages at your desired levels.) On the other hand, if the market is much down from its recent highs or has been and is still dropping quickly when you retire, take withdrawals for living costs out of your cash reserve for four years' worth of expenditures.

3. If the market is in a severe, long-term decline when you are taking withdrawals from your four-year cash reserve, keep doing so for an additional 18 months to two years to give the market time to rise significantly (the market almost always rises quickly during the first two years of an upmarket period), then switch back to taking withdrawals from your stock mutual funds. Return to live off of your stock mutual funds, and begin gradually building

back up your now noticeably depleted cash reserve to its needed level over 18 to 2 years. When the cash reserve has been completely refilled, you will be prepared for the inevitable next significant market slump.

Principle of asset allocation

1. The conventional mean-variance optimization (MVO) method of asset allocation is covered. We use this strategy in an "asset-only" context, where the objective is to construct the most effective combinations of asset classes in the absence of any liabilities. We include the main arguments against mean-variance optimization as well as solutions. Along with asset allocation, this section also discusses factor-based asset allocation, asset allocation with illiquid assets, and risk budgeting in connection to asset allocation. The following topic is brought up by the remark that practically all portfolios exist to

assist cover what would be considered a "liability."

2. presents liability-relative asset allocation, which includes the easy surplus optimization variation of mean-variance optimization. To determine the most effective asset class mixes when liabilities are present, surplus optimization is an economic balance sheet method that is applied to the liability side of the balance sheet. To evaluate the overall worth or health of the whole portfolio, liability-relative optimization takes into account both the return on the assets and the change in the value of the liabilities, in addition to how the assets and liabilities interact.

3. Goals-based asset allocation is a method of asset allocation that is becoming more and more common. Goal-based strategies analyze risk concerning certain demands or objectives linked with various time horizons

and levels of urgency, akin to liability-relative asset allocation in concept.

4. discusses several informal (heuristic) methods of determining asset allocations as well as other methods that emphasize certain goals.

5. The variables influencing decisions made while creating particular policies related to rebalancing to the strategic asset allocation are covered. Transaction costs, correlations, volatility, and risk aversion are some of the topics covered.

CHapter 10:
Cash in vs. cash out.

What is cash inflow.
The quantity of money flowing into your company is known as the cash inflow. When there is more money coming in than going out, there is a positive cash flow. Gains from an investment you made are included in cash inflow. It includes the cash you get right away from consumers in exchange for the goods or services you provide. Typically, this is the biggest component of cash inflow. Cash inflow is essential because it guarantees that your company operations will go as planned and that you will have enough money on hand to take the actions required for business expansion. Your company's ability to remain afloat and avoid bankruptcy is dependent on the flow of cash. It's not always the case that a healthy cash flow translates into increased profitability

What is cash outflow.

When money leaves your company, this is referred to as a cash outflow. When it comes to operations, cash outflow happens when you pay your workers' salaries and when you pay your rent. The amount you spend on fixed assets and the interest your company must pay on a loan it borrowed both counts as cash outflow. Negative cash flow occurs when cash outflow exceeds cash inflow; this is not a scenario you want to be in. Startups may initially have negative cash flows until their clients begin to purchase from them. The sooner your business's cash outflow starts to exceed its cash inflow, the better.

How to calculate cash flow

You can calculate cash flow with the following formula:

Net cash flow = Net cash flow from operating activities + Net cash flow from investing activities + Net cash flow from financial activities

Or

Net cash flow = Total cash inflows − Total cash outflows

It will be clear with a simple example. Let us say that a company called SunRays has calculated a net cash flow of $350,000 from operating activities, $50,000 from financial activities, and $5,000 from investment activities. The net cash flow would be as follows:

Net cash flow = $350,000 + $50,000 + $5,000

Net cash flow = $405,000

Note that if your business lost money due to an investment, then the investment amount will be written as a negative. For instance, if in the above example, SunRays lost $5,000 then the net cash flow would be $350,000 + $50,000 - $5000 which would equate to a net cash flow value of $400,000. In real life, cash flow calculations are much more complex because adjustments need to be made. For instance, income statement calculations are prepared on an accrual basis and so the amounts cannot be directly used to calculate cash flow.

What is cash flow, and why does business cash flow matters?

The net amount that enters and leaves your organization for some time is known as cash flow. Typically, this time frame is a month, quarter, or year. Operating operations, financing activities, and investment activities are the three main sources of cash flows. In other words, whenever your firm performs one of the three operations, cash flow—whether it comes into the business or out of the business—occurs. Depending on whether the cash inflow or outflow is bigger, the cash flow might be either positive or negative. Businesses must routinely check cash flow figures to make sure it is positive.

What is in the bank and supplier credit are not included in cash flow. It also excludes any sums that other parties owe your company. Simply put, cash flow is a measurement of how much money is coming into or going out of your firm during a certain period. Understanding your company's cash flow is crucial since investors and bank lenders use it to assess the financial health of your business. Businesses must continually monitor their cash flow because it reveals whether they can afford to buy the merchandise they need, pay their taxes, pay their employees, and cover their operating expenditures.

Types of Cash Flow

1. Operating
2. Investing
3. Financial

Operating Procedures

The term "cash flow from operational activities" describes the money that comes into or goes out of your company as a result of the production and sale of your goods and services, which constitute your normal business operations.

The net revenue you get through the sale of goods and services, inventories, and accounts receivable are all included in the inflow from operational operations.

In contrast, outflow describes the ongoing expenses of your company, including rent, sales and marketing expenses, income taxes, and staff salaries.

Investing Professions

The movement of funds related to the investments made by your organization is included in the cash flow from investing operations. You can make long-term investments like purchasing new machinery or structures or short-term ones like purchasing marketable securities.

Any investment acquisition is considered a cash outflow. In other words, in exchange for the investment, a particular quantity of money is leaving your company. Selling a long-term asset, such as a piece of machinery, results in a cash inflow.

The investment category frequently experiences more outflow than intake. Growing companies are more inclined to invest in long-term resources that promote expansion.

Financial Operations

The cash flow from financing operations, which includes stock sales, dividends, fundraising rounds, loans, and long-term debt repayments, is the last category.

Cash inflow in the financing area covers the sum you borrow as well as earnings from the sale of shares or equity. Dividend payments and money spent to pay off the principal on existing debt are both considered cash outflows.

You should be aware that the cash outflow for interest payments is represented as an operational activity rather than a financing activity.

Cash inflow vs cash outflow

Cash inflow

The net cash quantity that enters your organization and is readily available over time is known as cash inflow.

Customer payments, investment returns, and interest on loans you have granted to another firm are all examples of cash influx.

Cash outflow

The net cash amount that leaves your company because you are paying someone else or another organization is known as the cash outflow.

Cash outflow examples include money spent on fixed assets, wages, paying suppliers, taking out loans and paying interest on them, wages, transportation expenses, and insurance dividends that you must pay.

Chapter 11:
Cash safety net.

An insurance policy or a single savings account does not constitute a financial safety net. Instead, it consists of a wide range of risk-reduction strategies. A financial safety net is designed to shield you and your loved ones from losing your financial stability or failing to reach your long-term financial objectives, at least in part. This is especially true when an unplanned occurrence occurs, such as a sickness or a tragic personal incident.

Top five financial safety net.
1. Life Insurance

Life insurance is the most crucial financial safety net for your family when it comes to financial security. Although no one likes to discuss it, the truth is that you never know what will happen. Disaster may happen at any moment, regardless of your present state of health, your current financial situation, or your outlook for the future.

Unfortunately, your debt and outstanding debts do not go away after you pass away. Your family will need revenue to keep their standard of living intact.

The finest thing you can do is get life insurance to protect your family's financial future in the event of your passing. Here's how to determine if you need life insurance coverage.

Do you have any dependents—spouses, children, or others—who might face financial hardship in the event of your passing? Would they struggle to find enough money to continue paying their debts, the mortgage, and other expenses like health insurance? Would it be difficult for them to purchase enough food to last the day?

You must get life insurance if the answer is yes. Life insurance may help your family if you pass away suddenly and they lose all or a significant part of their monthly income.

Or, life insurance might help with bills like childcare and other home costs if your spouse has to start working.

Vantis Life offers a variety of insurance to help you protect the future of your family. Having the assurance that your family will be taken care of in the future will give you peace of mind now.

2. Emergency Reserve

Creating an emergency fund should be your next area of attention in terms of safety nets. Have you ever experienced an unforeseen expenditure for which you lacked the necessary funds? Perhaps your automobile broke down and required costly repairs, or perhaps you had an emergency and ended yourself in the hospital with high medical costs.

You can be forced to use high-interest credit cards if you don't have an emergency fund in place. In actuality, the typical interest rate on a credit card ranges from 15% to 23%. You'll have to pay a lot of interest, which is unfortunate.

You might also put off paying the bills in the hopes that they would disappear. However, doing so puts your loans in danger of being turned over to a collection agency. When this occurs, professional debt collectors are now pursuing you to get you to pay.

It's a lot of stress. However, credit bureaus will also get a record of it, which can harm your credit rating. These blemishes on your record may stay there for years and prevent you from getting new loans, like a mortgage or car loan.

It's crucial to have an emergency fund set up because of this. To ensure that you won't be tempted to use it, you should have at least $1,000 saved up in a separate savings account.

A better choice is to save up and put away three to six months' worth of income. In this manner, if you were to lose your job or were temporarily unable to work, you would have enough money to cover your expenses without having to forfeit your house or incur debt.

3. Insurance for Disability

If you become sick and can't work for a while, having long-term disability insurance may help. It's great to have a disability insurance policy in place even if you have an emergency fund so that you won't have to spend all of your resources when you are unable to work due to illness.

Having a handicap may affect anybody, at any age, even if it is more frequent among older individuals. Younger employees often get injuries from sports and auto accidents.

You also never know how long you could be out of a job. Though it could just last a few weeks, it might also last a year or more. You may not have nearly enough money even if you have an emergency reserve.

You could be fortunate enough to find employer-sponsored disability insurance coverage. Consider this a critical safety net to invest in as soon as you can, even if they don't.

4. Pension Accounts

Retiring as soon as feasible is everyone's goal.But the majority of individuals are not on the right route. In actuality, less than half of all American families have any savings for retirement.

Retirement plans are safety nets for the future even while they won't shield you from the present. It's critical to have enough money saved up before retirement age if you want to travel, spend time with your grandchildren, or start new activities after you retire.

Depending on your job status and income level, a wide range of tax-advantaged retirement plans are accessible. Contributions to these accounts should be made as much as possible each year by those who desire to put their financial stability first.

5. Having No Debt

The typical American owes more than $90,000 in debt, did you know that? Your mortgage, vehicle loan, school loans, and credit card debt are all cumulative. Additionally, these monthly payments are a significant hardship for most families because of increasing interest rates.

Being debt-free is one of the best safety nets to strive for and preserve. Consider the amount of money you might save each month if you were exempt from making any payments on your outstanding loan obligations.

Few things in life provide the mental tranquility that being debt-free does. To get out of debt as quickly as possible, do your best to create a budget, cut your monthly spending, and generate additional revenue. Create your financial safety nets now.

It's critical to begin creating your financial stability now. You need to put safety nets in place in advance since disasters and disabilities might happen at any moment.

Naturally, you hope you never need to use these resources. However, you'll be quite grateful to have them in place if you need to.

Consequences of not having a financial safety net

1. Make use of your paycheck

This probably won't concern you too much if your paycheck has enough wiggle space. If you can cover the expense by making just a few little adjustments to your monthly routines, great. If it means cutting down on evenings out or eating ramen a few times a week, wonderful for you.

2. Request a price break over many months.

Perhaps your profit margins are a little smaller or the expense is unusually high. Return to the firm in question in this situation, and have a conversation with them. They are often open to conversations about finding other means to pay off your debt, depending on your relationship with them and the nature of the expenditure. The fact that they get paid at the end of the day is what matters to them. You may spread out the expense more equally by paying in monthly installments rather than having to take a major financial blow all at once.

3. Get loans from family and friends

Everyone may not want to go with this. However, if you are lucky enough to be in a position where friends and relatives can assist you, think about contacting them to request assistance.

Our recommendation for obtaining a loan from family or friends is to properly discuss the conditions of repayment before accepting the loan. In certain circumstances, even creating and signing an informal agreement might help both parties understand its provisions. Make sure that paying back the loan you took out is your priority after covering your unexpected cost. Take the loan carefully since it's no secret that money can ruin even the most loving relationships. Avoid taking advantage of those you love or putting yourself in a situation where you owe more than you can afford to repay.

4. Cash advance

We can't claim that we entirely support this choice, hand on heart. If not repaid right away, payday loans, which feature some of the highest interest rates in the world of lending, may quickly trap you in a debt trap. They may be quite helpful if you are short on funds at a certain time but are very certain that you will have enough money to repay the loan in full soon. They are not a sensible choice, however, if you want to use them to tide you over until your next paycheck or if you won't have the money to pay them off soon.

Only choose this option if you are certain that you can pay off the loan in full within the grace period and that it won't trap you in a cycle of debt as you struggle to pay off enormous amounts of interest.

www.ingramcontent.com/pod-product-compliance
Lightning Source LLC
Chambersburg PA
CBHW050007230526
45465CB00003BB/1295